SURVEYING

T•H•E

LAND

Roots of Youth Ministry Series

This series addresses ecumenical and uniquely Presbyterian youth ministry concerns. Volumes in this series are intended for both professional and lay adults engaged in youth ministry.

Series Writers
Rodger Nishioka
Bob Tuttle
Lynn Turnage

Series Editor
Faye Burdick

Titles In Series

SURVEYING
T · H · E
LAND

LYNN TURNAGE

Bridge Resources
Louisville, Kentucky

Edited by Faye Burdick

Book interior and cover design by Pamela Ullman

First edition

Published by Bridge Resources
Louisville, Kentucky

Website address: http://www.pcusa.org/pcusa/currpub

PRINTED IN THE UNITED STATES OF AMERICA

97 98 99 00 01 02 03 04 05 06 — 10 9 8 7 6 5 4 3 2 1

Library of Congress Cataloging-in-Publication Data

Turnage, Lynn, date.
    Surveying the land / Lynn Turnage. — 1st ed.
        p.   cm. — (Roots of youth ministry series)
    Includes bibliographical references.
    ISBN 1–57895–008–2
    1. Church work with youth. I. Title. II. Series.
BV4447.T87 1997
259'.23—dc21   97-10160

This book is dedicated to the young people with whom I've worked and who have taught me so much, especially the youth of Black Mountain, North Carolina, and of Preston Hollow in Dallas and their families. I am grateful to all of you!

Special thanks to my parents, Mac and Anne—in a year they are retiring from salaried work, though they never have been and never will be retiring. I thank them for their encouragement, their challenges, and their teachings about gratitude and hospitality. I am also grateful for their constructive criticism, always encouraging me to look for a new and better way, and for their modeling and manifesting the love of Jesus Christ and the church.

Thanks also to teachers and role models who have helped me see how the pieces of life are connected, especially Judy Sutherland and Glenn Bannerman; to youth who have punched (and continue to punch) my buttons; and to friends who ask hard questions and challenge me to be more of the person God calls me to be.

I, Rodger Nishioka, and Bob Tuttle are especially grateful to Flora and Rick Hobson and their sons, David, Pat, and Cauley, for their gracious hospitality.

Contents

Introduction

Surveying the Land is more than looking at what you have. It's also planning for possibilities and laying the groundwork for growth. You don't have to be a "land professional" to "survey." Surveying the land is understanding the "land": the church, the youth, the culture in which the youth and church live. Surveying the land is also looking at where you want to be and planning how to get there.

Look up "survey" in a thesaurus or dictionary—it's a noun *and* a verb. The following words are all related to the word "survey," and they help explain what we will be doing in this book:

analysis	oversee	graph
examination	scan	map
perusal	examine	measure
investigation	inspect	appraise
poll	observe	ascertain
study	scrutinize	assess
overlook	chart	determine

In this book we will survey what we have and we will survey where we need to be. To help you begin and/or adjust and fine tune what your church is doing with youth ministry, we will look at the following:

- who youth are
- what the church is doing with or for youth
- what the church needs to do with or for youth
- how youth ministry is set up and how to get organized
- how all the pieces fit together
- how we communicate all this with the church and youth
- how we pay for youth ministry
- what the point is of all this surveying

As a leader of youth you need to get a clear idea of the landscape. One way to understand the lay of the land is to survey the landscape through reading the biblical Scriptures in the box on the next page.

1 Samuel 3
Jeremiah 1
Galatians 5:15–26
Ephesians 4:1–7
1 Corinthians 12
Acts 2

Take a Look at These Plots of Land

"It's a club! It's a clique! There's no Jesus-anything with those youth! Those youth don't even know who Jesus is! Why do we even have them here? We're pouring money into the deep hole called 'youth ministry'? What 'ministry' is happening down in that youth room anyway? All they ever do is play! What's supposed to be included in this so called ministry?"

1. What's wrong with this scene?
There are sixty-five youth between grades six and twelve on the rolls at First Presbyterian Church. In any given week, there are three to eight young people who come to eat, play basketball or some other sport, or go to a movie. Then they go home. What does this have to do with the church or faith?

2. What's wrong with this scene?
Fifteen out of twenty-five youth come every Sunday. They are the "best and the brightest," all eligible for community service awards at their high schools. They work at soup kitchens, do "rent-a-kid," or build Habitat houses every week.

3. What's wrong with this scene?
The Christian education committee is complaining that there is no balance, planning, or direction to the youth ministry program. The two youth advisors have no idea what "balance" or "planning" means. They help out because they like the young people and the young people like them. "A Big Brother–Big Sister program has more direction than our church's youth ministry program does," the committee complains.

4. What's wrong with this scene?

"We are so proud of our youth! They help in the nursery; they come to church every time the door is open; they are involved in the community; they participate in the life of the church. They will make great leaders of the church in the future."

5. What's wrong with this scene?

A parent calls the church to find out what time the lock-in is over. This parent dropped the youth at the church with a sleeping bag and a permission slip the night before. It's now 10 A.M. and the parent doesn't know what time to pick up the youth.

What are the assumptions here? Who are youth today? What do they need? What do they want? What *does* youth ministry really *look* like? Is it ministry *with* youth or ministry *for* youth?

What do we expect of our church's youth ministry? What is a balanced program? What does "balance" mean? How do we do planning? What do we already have in youth programming? And— my favorite question—*so what*?

Big church or little, small program or large, all of these questions are important. To begin to answer any of these questions we need to look at a primary premise: **Form Follows Function!** We get to the "whats" by looking at the "whys" and the "hows" first. We have to look at the functions of youth ministry and ask ourselves these questions and others, such as What do we have now? and What does our church need? When we answer these questions we start to discover the *function* of youth ministry. When we answer the question What is the intention of this ministry?, then we can move on to the *form*. How does all this take place and how do we plan for it?

Here we go. Let's look at all the pieces and the process by exploring the most often asked questions.

Who Are Our Youth?
What Are the Needs?

To understand the landscape, prepare yourself by surveying *Jeremiah 1:4–10* and *Luke 2:39–52.*

What do youth "look" like? What do they do with their free time? What is important to them? What are their joys and concerns?

In order to understand what to do with and for youth, we have to understand who youth are. Only then can we look at what they need. This is not a unique concept; in fact, it has its roots in theology. In all of Jesus' teachings and travels, and throughout his ministry with people, Jesus first assessed who the people were and what their needs were before doing anything. Jesus could do this quickly and easily. Once we know what we are looking at and looking for, we can do this too.

Most any person can tell us what they *want*, but it takes a different and deeper look at the situation, the culture, and the person to see what they really *need*. In working to understand what a person needs, we must first look at who they are. What makes them happy or sad? What do they think about? What motivates them both internally and externally?

Try the following exercise to help you better understand who youth are. This can be used in many different settings where youth and adults are together. The only supplies you need are newsprint (or other large pieces of paper), markers, and masking tape. Have your Bible open to *Luke 2:52* to read at the end of the exercise.

✦ An Exercise in Identity ✦

Remember those old posters from the 1970s and 1980s with a photograph of a "nerd" or a "jock" and labels for each part of their "uniform"? This exercise is to draw stick-figure versions of those posters, the subject being the youth in your church or the youth in the community who could be a part of the church. In the old posters, the jock or nerd wore everything that was characteristic of their stereotype: pocket protector and taped-up glasses for the nerds, helmets and shin guards for the jocks. Each item was labeled with its name and purpose.

Working in mixed groups of two to four adults and youth, draw a picture of youth and label everything the youth is wearing or thinking or dealing with. Have each group decide on the gender and age of the young person they will draw, and encourage them to give this person a name.

After they get started, ask them to illustrate what the person thinks and feels about the following:

School	Future
Parents	Church
Friends	God
Family	Clothes/Jewelry

Have the groups share their drawings and explain all the parts. After each group introduces their youth, have them tape their drawing to the wall.

Have the groups look at and share the commonalities and differences of the different youth in the drawings. Ask the following questions to make the discussion lively:

• What are the concerns of the different youth in the drawings?

• What are their joys?

• What are they interested in?

• What and whom do they care about? Why?

• What and whom do they not care about? Why not?

• What conclusions can be drawn about youth and their interests and needs?

This exercise should give all involved a look at who youth are and what they are interested in by lifting up some of the issues youth are facing, such as the following:

• cultural (material influences, cultural pressures)

• social (peer pressure, desire to fit in)

• emotional (joys and difficulties, desire to be accepted)

• physical (puberty; rapid, unpredictable physical changes)

• intellectual (school pressures, moving from concrete to abstract thinking)

• spiritual (seeking to experience the relevance of the faith and to make Jesus real)

Some of the good news for young people comes from the end of the birth narrative recorded in *Luke 2.* The chapter ends with the story of Jesus spending time in the Temple, teaching, learning, and doing what he wanted and felt called to do. The chapter ends, ". . . and Jesus increased in wisdom and in years, and in divine and human favor" *(Luke 2:52).*

The good news for young people is that the one we are to model has empathy for them too. Youth need to know that Jesus himself grew in wisdom (intellect), years (physical), divine favor (spiritual), and human favor (social). Youth today are dealing with these same issues. Jesus was *in* his culture, but not *of* his culture. Youth need to know they don't walk alone.

It used to be fairly predictable that the influences, concerns, and joys of young people revolved around family, church, school, and community. But today many of our youth live in two homes, go to church in two different places or maybe just once or twice a month, have friends in different schools, and often travel extensively (literally or figuratively, through such resources as the Internet). Their influences come from far and wide.

A basic premise of youth ministry today must be that we do youth ministry for the *whole* young person. The drawing exercise you did helps illustrate what you mean by identifying, to use a popular expression, what each youth brings to the table. And what they bring to the table is inevitably influenced, at least in part, by their family life. Because of this, and for the sake of discussions in this book, when we speak of youth ministry we are speaking of ministry related to *youth and their families.*

Issues of leadership are similar. It is important that both youth and adults be seen as leaders of the present youth program. These issues will be discussed with the Five Intentions of Youth Ministry in Chapter 3.

2

Where and Why Are Youth in the Church?

To understand the landscape, prepare yourself by surveying *1 Samuel 3* and *Jeremiah 1:4–10*.

Take a look at what you've got now. Whether it is one or two youth who are highly involved or a large group that is partially involved or somewhere in between, there is always room for improvement. There's nothing wrong with a little constructive criticism; it helps to take a look at what we do and makes sure it is being done well.

The problem comes when we sit back and rest on past accomplishments. Look over the next hill. What can be done better? What new challenges will we face when we climb that hill?

An Exercise in Involvement

If youth are in the church, ask yourself these questions:

• Where are they involved in the life of the church?

• Why are they there?

• What does that involvement do for them?

• What does that involvement do for the church?

If youth are *not* in the church, ask yourself why not.

• What keeps youth from coming?

• Is there something unattractive about this church?

• What is attractive about this church?

• Why would youth want to come?

• Why would youth not want to come?

There are strengths and weaknesses in any program. To keep an "edge" we need to look at these strengths and weaknesses and ask, Where is there room for improvement?

Evaluation and the process of evaluating says:
We want to practice what we preach.
We want to be who we say we are.
We care about the quality of what we are doing.
We want to be the best of who we are.

This is not a numbers game. Youth ministry is not about numbers, it's about being faithful. If we look at who we are as both a church and youth group and work to get the two in dialogue, we are trying to be faithful to our calling.

Assessing Your Youth Ministry

To start doing any of this we must first do two things: assess current youth ministry and determine the needs and interests of the youth. When that is done we need to see how those two things line up. Are some needs and interests not being addressed? Most likely the answer is yes. So what needs to be tweaked to get youth to benefit more from the ministry of the church?

A youth council is a group of youth and adults working together to assess, plan, implement, and evaluate the ministries that are offered to youth in the local church. Whether you call it a youth council or a youth committee, the group that oversees what happens with the youth is what we are addressing. With the Presbyterian Youth Connection, many are referring to their youth council as Presbyterian Youth Council (PYC) or Presbyterian Youth Connection Council (PYCC).

To get to the assessment, there are several places in the church to begin exploring and collecting information. These gathering settings include the following: session, session committees, Christian education committee, youth with an advisor, youth with a staff member or other volunteer, individual youth, staff members, parents of current and future youth participants.

It is important that *at least* two of these groupings of people be involved in this process. All of these segments of the church community can be included in assessment of what is happening with your church's youth ministry. It is also important to include people who participate in different aspects of the current program and/or are interested in future programs. Information you should collect from these various sources includes the following:

- **Ages/grades**—the "demographics" of each age group. (To plan a senior high program when the oldest youth is currently in the sixth grade is not helpful.)
- **Numbers** of involved and potentially involved youth. (Look at the number of children coming up through grade school and the number of youth in the surrounding communities who may be attracted to a strong youth program.)
- **Schools** represented by the involved youth. (Programming for youth who all go to the same school is not the same as programming for youth who go to several different schools.)
- **Places** of involvement, both in church and community. (This shows any variety in interests and commitment among youth.)
- **Desires** for the future.
- **Concerns** or issues that need to be addressed by the program.
- **Staffing** issues, suggestions, or concerns.
- **Dreams** for the focus of the program. (What should this church's youth ministry look like in five years?)

Take a look at the gathered data. Consider that in any gathering of information, the top 10 percent and the bottom 10 percent of the information is considered "extreme." Disregard the best of the best comments and the worst of the worst comments.

Once this is done, you can ask yourself the following:

What conclusions can be drawn?

Who is being served?

Who is not being served?

What needs to be deleted?

What needs to be added?

What needs to be changed?

On the following pages are several forms you can photocopy and use to help you collect information and use it to evaluate your youth ministry program.

Questionnaire on Youth Ministry

Date: _____

Who are you? [check *all* that apply]

❑ Youth   ❑ Youth church school teacher

❑ Parent of youth   ❑ Member of _____ committee

❑ Session member   ❑ Staff member

❑ Youth advisor   ❑ Other _____

How long have you participated in this church? _____

Number of youth in your family: _____

Age/grades of the youth: _____

School you attend (if you are a youth): _____

Programs in your church designed specifically for youth: _____

    each week: _____

    each month: _____

    each quarter: _____

    each year: _____

If you are a youth, name the church programs in which you participate.

    each week: _____

    each month: _____

    each quarter: _____

    each year: _____

Programs you'd like to see happen with youth: _____

If you are a youth, name other church programs you would participate in in the life of the church: _____

Five years from now I hope our church's youth ministry _____

One more thing I'd like to say about this church and youth programs is

_____

_____

_____

Collating the Information

Dates information was collected: _____

Numbers of youth on the rolls: _____

Ages or grades of youth on the rolls: _____

Number of youth currently attending youth ministry programs: _____

Ages or grades of youth currently attending youth ministry programs:

Schools represented by youth: _____

Programs in your church in which youth participate: _____

Designed specifically for youth: _____

    each week: _____

    each month: _____

    each quarter: _____

    each year: _____

Designed for anyone in which youth participate: _____

    each week: _____

    each month: _____

    each quarter: _____

    each year: _____

Other youth program possibilities: _____

Other church program possibilities: _____

Hopes for the youth ministry program five years from now: _____

Other comments: _____

Evaluation Tool

This page will be helpful for both evaluating current programs and preparing for future programs. Ask youth involved in the program and other youth and adults related to the youth ministry of the church to complete the chart.

Answer the following questions below and then translate those occasions to the appropriate portion of the chart on page 10.

1. What has been the most fun about the youth activities?

2. What have you learned in youth activities? When has been the best time to learn?

3. Describe a time that was worshipful for you during a youth activity.

4. Give an example of when the youth program helped someone other than youth.

Location	1. Recreation	2. Study	3. Worship	4. Service
At Church				
Away from Church				

What Is the Intention
of Youth Ministry?

To understand the landscape, prepare yourself by surveying *Acts 2:1–4, 32–47* and *Ephesians 4:11–16.*

Basic youth ministry is built on five basic directions, functions, and claims, known as the Five Intentions of Presbyterian Youth Ministry. Youth ministry is

1. To call young people to be disciples of Jesus Christ

2. To respond to the needs and the interests of young people

3. To work together, youth and adults, in partnership

4. To be connected to the whole church, community, and world

5. To include all young people, reaching out and inviting them to belong to the community of faith.

These Five Intentions very simply imply that we

- Are proudly Christian. Everything we do is in response to our faith in Jesus Christ, and we encourage youth to explore what this means and how we live this out.

- Help youth realize they are children of God, and that identity permeates all we are and do.

- Help youth know they are welcome and belong in this family of God called "church." Youth need to know that no matter where they come from or what they've experienced, they have a place in the church.

- Know who young people are and work to include their needs and interests in our programming, always challenging them to hold these up to the life and witness of Jesus Christ.

- Help youth discover their God-given gifts and talents and help them see how these gifts are connected to other people and need to be shared.

- Work with youth. Programming does not happen *for* young people. Young people are *involved* in decisions made about what happens with them.

- Realize that youth are not only the church of tomorrow, they are the church of *today* too! They have a role and a place in leadership and on committees right now. Youth *are* leaders. We need to look for ways to encourage and nurture youth in leadership. Leading in partnership with adults is one way that youth in leadership can come alive.

• Help youth see how they are connected to each other and the entire world. Youth ministry cannot be a satellite program. It cannot be a place where we put youth in a holding pattern and wait for them to "get over" this stage of their development before they join the life of the church and the world. Youth ministry must be a part of the whole.

• Encourage youth to see themselves *and participate* in this place where faith and life cannot be separated. Youth need to see how and where faith is connected to life and that the life Christ calls us to is life that happens every day beyond the walls of the church.

• Exclude no one. There is no reason why *all* people cannot be welcome in the life of any youth program or church. This community of faith is living and breathing and therefore open.

The material in this chapter relates to the Presbyterian Youth Connection (PYC) for the Presbyterian Church (U.S.A.). Also see the Vision Statement for Youth Ministry in the Presbyterian Church (U.S.A.), found in the Appendix.

The Vision Statement is a kind of "purpose statement" for youth ministry. It has been adopted by many youth councils and local churches to help guide and direct local church youth ministry. The Vision Statement and the Five Intentions can also function as a check-and-balance system for what is done with and for youth in any church situation. For any planning session or event, the question is

• How does this event measure up to the Five Intentions and the Vision Statement?

To put it another way,

• Does this activity make the Five Intentions or the Vision Statement come alive?

Therefore we need to

Assess	Balance
Respond	Plan
Discover	Connect
Involve	Challenge

All the pieces are here for examining the church and the youth. Plan accordingly. It should be possible to use these Five Intentions to make your church's mission statement come alive for the youth of the congregation. Likewise, anything we do or use with youth and youth ministry in the local church needs, in some way, to reflect these Five Intentions.

Where and How Do We Get a Youth Council?

To understand the landscape, prepare yourself by surveying *Ecclesiastes 3:1–15* and *Matthew 4:18–22*.

The title of this chapter may have you asking yourself, Can we do this? Can it really work? It can. The examples and procedures discussed in this chapter have all been implemented in different places around the country. It is possible to scale down or expand any of the following to suit your situation.

Why Have a Youth Council?

Youth councils bring to life all of the Five Intentions of Youth Ministry, especially the third Intention: "Work together, youth and adults, in partnership." They also

- are a way of organizing and involving youth in their own ministry with and for the youth of the church;

- are a means of accountability, checking to see that the Five Intentions are being carried out and the Vision Statement for Youth Ministry is happening;

- make sure details are being covered and procedures are followed.

Note to small churches or churches with small youth groups:
If your entire youth group can fit in a single car, you may want to have the whole group function as a youth council. They can meet as a council several times a year for planning purposes.

Who Makes Up the Youth Council?

Any youth council needs to be a representative group, so think about who needs to be represented from your church in order to carry out a well-rounded youth ministry. Ideally, a youth council will function like a session or a microcosm of a session. There are

- representatives from different ages of youth (middle school, junior high, high school)

- representatives from different interest groups (morning church school, evening youth group, special events and fundraisers, curriculum, recruitment)
- adults who are advocates for youth (parents, advisors, teachers, parents of younger children)
- representatives of both genders
- people with different gifts (organizers, brainstormers, idea people, detail people)
- committees or subcommittees that do work outside the youth council meeting and report back (church school committee, youth group committee)

The cochairs of the youth council ideally are a youth and an adult. It is also desirable that the adult or youth be an active elder. The term of service for the chairs is a full year. To spread the leadership among the youth, or in the event a youth cochair cannot serve a full year, you can rotate the cochair youth position every quarter or every six months. In the ideal situation—where the adult cochair is an active elder—it also helps with continuity if this person can serve as cochair for the year and have this renewable annually for as long as his or her term of service on the session.

What Do They Do?

Think about the session of your church. The youth council can function as a microcosm of the session, making plans for the youth of the church and making sure committee work is done.

Youth council committees can be grouped like session committees as well. Look at your own church and use that as a model. If you think there is room for improvement, make some changes to the model and use it for the youth council. Here are some possible groupings for responsibilities of youth council committees:

- Sunday evening (youth group/Presbyterian Youth Council meetings)
- Sunday morning (church school)
- Special events (fundraisers, camps and conferences, mission projects)
- Recruitment (getting volunteers for long-term [six months or more] commitments)

In this model, each group is responsible for its own curriculum, and the calendar and leadership needs are coordinated by the youth council as a whole.

Another possible grouping might be:

- Education (Sunday morning church school and Sunday evening fellowship)
- Mission projects (service done with and for others)
- Fundraisers

The youth council then functions as a coordinating body for all of these pieces and their interplay.

The youth council as a whole needs to meet every four to six weeks to check on details of the different committees and coordinate all their work. In the spring of each year a major brainstorming event or retreat could be held to plan the work of the youth council and youth programming for the next twelve to eighteen months.

How Long Do They Serve?

A youth council member can serve twelve to eighteen months. Terms should begin in January and conclude the next December or the following July. There should be a limit to the number of consecutive terms that can be served—two to three for youth and adults alike, although it may be possible for an adult to serve as many as four terms.

Length of Service
Eighteen-month term
Advantages

- Anyone new to the youth council has about four to six months to get their feet wet and get into the swing of the work of the council.
- There is good continuity between youth councils from year to year.
- High school seniors on the youth council can serve until they get out of high school.
- The rotation is clear for youth: they rotate on in the middle of a traditional school year and rotate off before starting another school year.
- There is a broad and clear planning cycle and a chance to plan ahead and plan for detail.
- There is a large group to brainstorm and plan the next year of youth ministry.
- If someone cannot fulfill their term, the work of the council is not interrupted because of the broad planning cycles that eighteen-month commitments allow.

Eighteen-month term
Disadvantages

- The potential is there for the youth council to be very large for about six months of each year (January to June).
- The system and timing of rotating on and off can be strange for the adults or those not on a traditional school-year calendar.
- It appears to be a commitment to a long term.

Twelve-month term
Advantages

- The cycles can begin in August or September with the traditional school-year calendar, at the start of the calendar year, or even in April.
- It is easy to commit to a twelve-month cycle.

Twelve-month term
Disadvantages

- Planning ahead is not as clear because the current youth council is planning for a year they may not be a part of.
- Continuity between the makeup of the youth council from year to year can be scattered and it may therefore take the council a few months to pull things together each time a change in membership occurs.

Looking at needs of the youth in the church, brainstorming ideas, implementing these ideas, evaluating all aspects of youth ministry—all of this happens at the initiative of the youth council.

Think in terms of the cycles of the year. When is it best to brainstorm and plan, and when is it best to work on details?

Winter

- New elders join session committees.
- Orientation for new adults on youth council can happen now.
- Great programming possibilities can happen to help avert "winter blahs."

Spring

- Appoint new youth council members (right after any changes in the session and session committees are made).

- Make catchy titles for youth activities to entice youth to come to regularly scheduled events.

- Evaluate the last year, or at least the last six months, of your youth ministry program.

In the mid- to late spring

- Have a planning meeting or retreat with the youth council.

In the late spring and through the summer

- Plan for the next year. (Work on details of big events, decide what adult help may be needed, make sure there are events on the calendar, make sure names of responsible parties are beside each event.)

In the late spring and through the summer, if necessary

- Solicit adult help for the program. (Enlist teachers and advisors who can commit to a year of service beginning in the fall.)

☼ Summer ☼

- Do experimental programs and risk some new ideas. (People are usually open to the new and different kinds of programming during some of the more relaxing times of the summer months.)

- Publicize highlights of the coming year.

In the late summer

- Have a parent–youth event to look at the coming year and get events on family calendars.

- Solicit parent help for extra drivers, cooks, and so forth.

🍁 Fall 🍁

- Kick off the youth programming year at the start of the traditional school year. (Do something new, big, and exciting to get the youth and their families on board with the new year of programming for youth in the church.)

In the fall and early winter

- Youth enjoy the new routines of youth ministry activities. There are lots of holiday and liturgical possibilities for special programs.

How Are Council Members Picked?

All youth council representatives, no matter how they are selected, must be approved by the session. There are several ways the youth council makeup can be established:

1. Youth council members can be appointed by the youth council and/or session of the church working in conjunction with the church staff.

2. The youth council can be nominated and elected into the appointments by the youth of the church.

3. Youth members of the council can be elected and the adult members can be appointed by the session, the nominating committee, or an executive committee of youth, adults, and church staff.

How Do They Work?

The youth council takes the work of the planning process, which will be explained in Chapter 6, and makes it come alive. Therefore this group must be organized to reflect and help implement this work. The organization of the youth council is a form that follows the functions laid out by the planning process.

It would be helpful to have this group of people look at the following documents as they think about and discuss how they will function:

• Their church's mission statement

• The Five Intentions of Presbyterian Youth Ministry (See Chapter 3 and p. 60 in the Appendix)

• The Vision Statement for Youth Ministry in the Presbyterian Church (U.S.A.) (See p. 61 in the Appendix)

• The Purpose Statement for Presbyterian Youth Connection, and any other "purpose"-type documents from the local church

Then this group needs to ask itself, How do we need to be structured to make these purpose statements come alive? How do the activities we do and have planned reflect these purpose statements? How can these pieces be grouped into working groups or committees, or subcommittees, to help us function effectively for our church and situation?

Some suggested subcommittees include church school/curriculum, youth group/fellowship, special events, and recruitment.

It is wise to keep the number of subcommittees to a minimum. It may be counterproductive to have six or eight subcommittees—the work of the people gets spread thin and the reporting time in a youth council meeting gets long.

Youth council subcommittees take the work of the planning process and get the details done. They either do the work themselves or make sure it is parceled out to others to do. Then the youth council will work to coordinate the work of all the subcommittees.

1. It is up to the youth council to determine how often it needs to meet to get their work done. Some meet as often as every four weeks, while others can get the work done and meet every six to eight weeks.

2. When the youth council meets, someone needs to take minutes. This responsibility can be rotated among the members. The cochairs of the youth council can be responsible for circulating the minutes. If traditional minutes are not taken, council members need to spend a few moments at the end of the meeting recounting and writing down all the decisions that were made and reports that were given. Some form of record keeping should be established.

3. The youth council should also decide what material needs to be publicized before the next meeting, and who is responsible for getting that material out to the other youth.

4. A special notation of "youth issues" at the end of the youth council minutes can be *very* helpful in informing the Christian education or nurture committees and the session or other people who might read the minutes. This information can help others understand who youth are and what they are dealing with today and what it means for the youth in their church. Simple comments can be educational and informative—it may even be helpful to quote some youth experts, philosophers, and psychologists, among others. This information must be true and relevant to make this helpful and trusted. Examples include the following:

   • "Adolescents are moving from concrete to abstract thinking," said Jean Piaget. This means we need to encourage youth to explore the traditional symbols of the faith and encourage them to create and explain their own.

   • "The biggest pressure I have is to make good grades." If parents and church encourage this pressure, youth will come to believe that love is conditional instead of unconditional. Youth need to be encouraged to be the best of who God calls them to be.

- The Youth Treasure Hunt is our church's big kickoff for the year. Please encourage youth you know to attend!

- Our church's youth will be on a mission trip building a school during spring break. Please pray for their safe travels, their work, and for a great experience of faith coming alive.

How Do You Evaluate the Youth Council and the Work It Does?

All work that the youth council does needs to be held up against the church's mission statement, the Five Intentions for Youth Ministry, and any vision statement or mission statement that the youth council may have. So, no work or ministry is done that has not first passed that test.

In addition, before any planning for the coming year is done it is helpful to do at least one of the two following kinds of evaluations of past programs:

1. The youth council can evaluate on its own. They should spend some time talking about the best and most difficult parts of the past year, both programmatically and as related to the work of the youth council.

2. The council can initiate an evaluation that is sent to the youth and their families asking questions (open-ended or multiple choice) related to both the work of the youth council and the youth ministry programs of the church. This evaluation can be part of a larger assessment, as referred to in Chapter 2, or can stand on its own.

To Whom Should the Council Report?

The youth council can report to the Christian education committee of the session, or the closest facsimile thereof. (In my dreams, the youth council reports straight to the session. If this happens in your church, consider yourself extremely blessed!) Someone from the youth council needs to sit on this oversight committee, be it Christian education or otherwise.

Therefore, any of the following types of decisions made by the youth council need to be reported to the oversight committee and then to the session for any appropriate approvals. These include issues related to:

policy
budgets
vision statements
recruitment of leaders
allocation of major amounts of money
overall schedules

With Whom Does the Council Connect ?

This is probably obvious at this point: the youth and everyone connected to them (families, teachers, leaders, other youth) relate to the youth council and vice versa. The youth council relates to the oversight committee. Any issues related to the youth and youth council that come in from another committee or group in the church should come in through the youth council by way of the youth council cochairs.

The youth council can be the vehicle to help youth get involved in other aspects of the church. The council can help appoint or recommend youth to work in other places within the church. There is no reason why youth cannot be integrated into all committees of the church. The key will be getting them on committees that are related to their interests and abilities and making sure they are encouraged to participate in the life of those committees.

It will be helpful if all requests for youth's help in other places in the life of the church come through the youth council. There are some issues and events that are related to the life of the church that may or may not be appropriate for youth to be involved with. For example, the youth may want to help clean up after the all-church Christmas party as a way of serving the church. But if this is the only opportunity youth are given to be involved in this particular event, it may be seen as tokenism. Tokenism does not encourage youth to be integral parts of the life of the church. Instead, it often makes them feel like second-class citizens.

The notes at the end of the youth council minutes are also a place where information that has to do with other committees and areas of the church can be shared. This is a good way to encourage interconnectedness within the church.

5

What Is a Balanced Program?

To understand the landscape, prepare by surveying *Matthew 5:1–12*.

To help fulfill the Five Intentions of Presbyterian Youth Ministry, a ministry must be planned with four elements in mind: **recreation**, **study**, **worship**, and **service**. Each of these may be subdivided, but it's easier to plan with these four in mind.

We must have *a balance* of all of these elements. Balance means that

- in any given chunk of time, each of these elements happens—every evening in some months, every Sunday in some months, but at least every month and quarter and certainly every year;

- no one of these elements takes over and drives the programming of the youth ministry; and

- each of these elements can happen within any given time period, whether it is a single event or evening, a month of programming, or an entire quarter or year of the calendar.

To balance these activities implies that

- we plan and do events that are a reflection of all of the Five Intentions of Presbyterian Youth Ministry;

- we do not have an overabundance of any one type of activity in any given period of time;

- we have a calendar of events that are planned; and

- we realize that balance does not mean doing all of these things all of the time! It does mean that if we were to look at the whole youth program over a given period of time, we could call it holistic.

Holistic implies that

- there is a whole view of everything that is done;

- all parts are important—no one aspect of the whole is greater or more important than another; and

- both people and programs are considered in the planning.

So how do we *balance* and plan *holistically*? Remember, the Five Intentions must be reflected in all of this.

Within the church or community of faith, these elements of youth ministry programming take place. See next page for elements and general definitions.

Recreation Is

- activities that build up individuals and bring the community together
- fun
- fellowship
- a place and time to share joy or sorrow
- community building—it does not make fun of individuals or make any person or group of people feel awkward
- inclusive of all abilities and interests

Study Is

- learning
- studying a specific topic, theological concept, biblical character or idea, or faith and life issue
- exploring a new concept or idea
- understanding someone or something better or in a new and different light

Worship Is

- formal or informal
- prayer
- not tied to a particular location or time
- praising God
- listening to God
- celebrating God's goodness in our lives
- motivation to continue to do the work of our Lord Jesus Christ

Service Is

- helping others
- learning about others
- working with people
- serving a need
- selfless giving
- done for the glory of God

Obviously there is integration and overlap between each of these elements. It is possible to be recreated in worship, worship during recreation, study during service, and so on. But do *not* assume that young people—or other adults for that matter—understand these kinds of integration issues. We've got to open the door to help them understand what all the pieces are and how they are connected.

Some Examples

If you close an evening of volleyball with a devotion, it will help if you can do two things: (1) find something in the volleyball play *(recreation)* to relate to the Bible *study*—an analogy, something someone did or shared; and (2) ask the youth what they learn from playing volleyball at youth group as opposed to playing it at school or some other place.

If the event is on *worship*, make it fun and engaging *(recreational)*. It is also possible to *serve* others by helping them have a good time, such as babysitting and playing with children so their parents can go Christmas shopping.

Also, studying *recreation* can be *study* and recreational. Studying worship can be worshipful while still teaching about *worship*.

Studying missions or *service* can be helping people and talking about how that was a service. Service can have a *worship* element if the *service* is commissioned, or if there is a worship dedicating the work to the glory of God.

Who Plans All This?

According to the Five Intentions, youth and adults *together* do planning. If the youth group is small, the whole group can do the planning. Even if the youth group is large, the first several steps can be done with the youth group as a whole and can then be turned over to the youth council or other committees to be completed and implemented.

It is also possible that the list of possibilities for study can be lengthened to be used for all youth events, with some of the ideas related to study being turned over to those working with church school.

Before you move on to the next chapter, it is assumed that

- the youth and adults doing the planning *know* the needs and interests of the young people that the program is to serve

- there is a youth council of some kind that can continue to work through this process even after the initial planning meeting.

6

How Do You Do Planning and Programming?

To understand the landscape, prepare yourself by surveying *Psalm 139:1–18* and *Mark 4:13–20*.

Throughout the entire planning process, the youth and others involved must keep in mind all of the places that this programming can take place. Think about the physical space that is available. In situations where you have the privilege of dreaming future spaces, think practically and think beyond the current opportunities.

The following design can be modified to fit into a two-hour block, but it will fit most comfortably into a four-hour format with a break after two hours. The program can easily be lengthened or elaborated upon for use at an all-day youth council retreat or a weekend planning event.

A Planning Process for Youth

Before this event begins, it will be important to decide what person or persons facilitate this process. It can be a single person who takes the time to read this material and who can move the group forward, or it can be led by youth and an adult, or two adults, or two youth. More than two or three leaders will get cumbersome.

Also, the youth council or other organizing group will need to decide the following ahead of time:

- Who is this planning for? (all youth, broadly graded, only junior high or middle school, only senior high)

- What time period are you planning for? (three to six months, twelve to eighteen months)

- How far do you need to get? (generate ideas, mark events on calendar, assign tasks)

- Who is involved in this process? (Much of this can be done by any interested parties—youth, adults, parents—but it is imperative that the *youth* are involved in this process. It *cannot* be done for them by interested adults. The youth council can begin the process and open it to any wider representation of youth.)

- What is the time frame for this planning? (two hours, four hours, a day, a weekend)

This process can be used to plan for the short term—three to six months—or for looking ahead a year to eighteen months. With some adjustments in the Stating the Purpose portion, this plan can be used to help a church look at needs for the future—including building and facility needs—as they relate to the growth and development of the youth program. If this is done, it would be most helpful to have representation from the session involved in this process.

Overview of Process for Youth Programming

1. Beginning and Preparation
2. Group Building
3. Stating the Purpose
4. Defining the Elements of a Balanced Program
5. Brainstorming
6. Prioritizing
7. Marking the Calendar
8. Balancing the Schedule
9. Closing

1. Beginning and Preparation

Open room with space to move. Chairs are not necessary.

Materials Needed

- Sheets of paper, cardstock, or construction paper for calendar and puzzle pieces
- Newsprint for graffiti sheets and program headings
- 3" x 5" (7.5 cm x 12.5 cm) or 4" x 6" (10 cm x 15 cm) cards for events that will go on the calendar
- Markers—four different colors, one for each program heading
- Calendars that are available (church events, local school schedules, etc.)
- The Five Intentions of Presbyterian Youth Ministry (post on wall, p. 60)
- A Vision for Presbyterian Youth Ministry (post on wall, p. 61)

In Advance

Prepare a calendar by writing the months of the year (September through September, or whatever time frame you are planning for) on sheets of paper, one sheet for each month, and place them on the walls around the room. Write dates that are not negotiable, such as Christmas and Easter, on the calendar now. Then put each "given" event on a card and tape the cards to the calendar. These "given" events might include church retreats, a hunger walk, holidays, mission projects, and other activities already in the works for the church.

Program Elements

Write the following headings on the top of a sheet of newsprint, one heading per sheet:

Recreation
Study
Worship
Mission

Put these near each other on the wall.

Puzzle Pieces for Group Building

Put the following words on paper, one per sheet: Recreation, Study, Worship, Mission. Then cut each sheet of paper into enough pieces so that there is one piece for everyone. Construction paper works well for this.

Beginning

Put pieces of paper or newsprint on the floor with the following questions written on them:

- What's your favorite thing to do when you have free time?
- What is a part of worship?
- How can worship happen?
- What question do you have about your faith?
- What are some concerns you have about your life? about your faith? about school or church?
- What is recreation? Why should we do recreation at church?
- What do you like to do at church?

As participants arrive, invite them to write answers to the questions on the graffiti sheets.

2. Group Building

After a few participants have arrived, hand out puzzle pieces cut from the construction paper. Ask the group members to trade pieces until you give them a signal to stop. Encourage participants to work together to make a whole puzzle. The four puzzles should form the words recreation, study, worship, and mission.

After these four small groups have gotten together, ask them to discuss among themselves a hope they have for the church's youth program. Tell them this is the group they will work with for the next period of time.

Give the groups the sheet of newsprint that corresponds to their puzzle piece (recreation, mission, worship, or study).

With early adolescents, (middle schoolers), make sure you have an adult in each group.

3. Stating the Purpose

After adequate time for discussion, gather all participants together and have them sit on the floor. Open with prayer for this process, asking for God's guidance. Discuss the purpose of the event by pointing out the four elements of a balanced program. Ask the group why a balanced program is important. Reiterate that balance needs to happen over a month, a quarter, and the whole year.

Explain that this process will lead to putting *their* ideas on the calendars on the walls. Tell the group how far you hope to get during this time period.

If an evaluation of the church's youth program has already been done or if data has already been gathered, now is the time to peruse this information. Divide up the information and have the groups go through it, making notes of ideas or comments that were heard several times and any other valid issues that may need to be discussed.

This is also the time to note the church's vision statement and Five Intentions for Presbyterian Youth Ministry. If there are new people in the group, tell them where these came from and what their purposes are.

4. Defining the Elements of a Balanced Program

Take five minutes and have the group define the words that were on the wall: recreation, study, worship, and mission.

Ask each group to come up with a brief description of the word they have on their puzzle piece. Explain to youth that this is their group whose task is defining their word in order to have a meaning that the larger group can use for planning purposes. Explain to the groups that they will have input into the other areas, but this is the group they will be working with during this process. Tell them they will be sharing their definitions of their word with the other groups. Encourage them to reflect on or compare what they come up with with what they wrote on the graffiti sheets when they came in. Give them another sheet of paper or newsprint to write their definition on. After a few minutes ask each group to share its definition. Invite the other groups to add any other information or clarify the definitions. Then have them post their definitions above their corresponding words on the wall.

5. Brainstorming

Ask, What is brainstorming?

Tell participants that they have been given a sheet of newsprint with their word on it. They are to brainstorm ideas that come to mind for that category. There are *no* wrong answers in brainstorming! If an idea comes out of someone's mouth, it goes on the sheet. Youth need to write legibly but not too big—there needs to be room on the paper for lots of ideas.

Depending on the group, you may need to do a "covenant check" at this point or have some kind of agreement so that ideas are reasonable, semi-realistic, and helpful. (A covenant is a solemn promise made between persons and with God.) Every youth program is encouraged to develop a covenant at least annually, and should consider doing a Bible study on covenants and their purposes. Covenants often have to do with conduct and expectations about interactions within a group. A "covenant check" is a phrase that can be used by anyone in a group to check the covenant and its contents and implications. This phrase usually means that all conversations and actions stop and the group checks on these issues before continuing. This also helps with issues of confidentiality, ownership, fairness, honesty, and so on. Put-downs and comments that leave anyone out will not be productive or helpful.

Give the groups three minutes to come up with all the ideas they can for their topic. After three minutes, switch sheets—pick up one sheet, pass it to another group, pick up that group's sheet and pass it to the next group, and so on. Give groups three minutes on this next topic. Explain that they are to read what was written by the previous group and brainstorm more ideas to add to it. Do this passing procedure until they get their original topic back.

6. Prioritizing

When groups get their original topic back, tell them they are beginning to move out of the brainstorming process. They can keep adding ideas, but mostly they will begin to remove ideas. It is important at this point to emphasize to the group that ideas are ideas. Participants cannot expect that any particular idea that goes on the sheet will automatically be a program that the church will do. "Give it up" is the phrase to use. At this point, if an idea gets removed, it can still be put back on the list as the sheet comes around. But it is important that everyone realize that ideas belong to the group and the process and not to any one individual.

Tell participants they should now *add and delete* items. They can begin to delete items that are too expensive, take too much time, are something they don't like, or are ideas that exclude certain groups or people. Issues of stewardship and inclusivity need to be considered. You may need to do a covenant check and delete some inappropriate topics at this point. Participants have three minutes per sheet in this part of the process too.

After three minutes on a sheet, pass the sheets again. From this point on they need to *add*, *delete*, and *star*. *Star* means to put a star or some other symbol next to three activities on the sheet they are working with. These should be three activities that they would *really* like to do. This is a way of voting. This time around, give only two minutes per sheet to *add*, *delete*, and *star*. Again, groups should pass the sheets until they get their original back. Explain that any topic can be starred more than once.

You as leader need to be responsible for keeping time and passing the sheets, so that the youth and adults can concentrate on ideas.

When they get their original topic back, tell each group to add, delete, and star one last time on their sheet.

Give the groups eight to ten blank cards. Tell them to pick the top eight to ten activities from their sheet and put one on each card.

After they have had five to ten minutes to complete this, ask the groups to share with the whole group their Top Ten list.

Since "form follows function," the next step is to look at all of the activities and try to balance the month, quarter, and year with the four elements (recreation, study, worship, and mission).

Next the group should look at the time and places in which each month's activities could happen. Decide the amount of time needed for each activity. Does it happen at church school, Sunday evening, mid-week, a long weekend, or some other time? Make these notes on the cards for each activity.

Ask the groups to post their newsprints. If the original sheet is illegible, ask them to rewrite their Top Eight to Ten ideas on another sheet of newsprint. Don't throw out the old lists, you may need more of those old ideas.

7. Marking the Calendar

Direct each group to take ideas now on cards and put them in the months of the year in which they want their events to take place, using the calendar months hung on the walls around the room. They will begin to see that their "Top Ten" may need to be enlarged to fill the calendar. Or if the program is not large, a Top Ten list may be too much for one year, and the groups will find that doing a Top Five from each category is plenty.

Each group is responsible for putting their cards on the calendar month around the room, taking into account the need for balance over the entire year (or for however long you are planning).

As they finish their group's cards, have each person go around to the cards and write their initials beside any item on any list that they would like to *help lead or organize!*

From this point on, it is possible for the youth council to take the responsibility for making sure the information is disseminated and put into the right hands to get the jobs completed.

Other Options at the Calendar Phase

1. Have each group put their Top Eight ideas under their heading on the wall. Then have the youth council or a representative group of youth and advisors place them on the calendar.

2. Assign a heading to each Sunday of the month—Recreation, Study, Worship, or Mission—and have the youth put their subjects on their days of the month. The youth group or youth council will then have to edit and rearrange a bit to make sure the month or quarter flows and has a realistic look and balance to it.

3. Have the groups place their Top Eight across the calendar, spreading out their topic over the year. The group or youth council must then do an edit to check out the balance and flow of activities. Is there a balance between activities in house and those out of the church? Is the cost of events reasonable and spread out across the church? Are the energies required for planning particular events balanced? Is there a "series" that may need to be put together on consecutive Sundays or within a particular time slot (e.g., sex education, parent/youth series, etc.)?

Dates

If it is not already done, establish and put on the calendar the day of the week or month for the regularly scheduled Presbyterian Youth Council meetings. Looking at all this programming, decide how often and when you want and need the youth to meet. Should it be

✓ every Sunday night?

✓ Wednesday evenings?

✓ every other Saturday?

✓ weekly?

✓ monthly?

✓ bimonthly?

✓ regularly scheduled retreats?

✓ presbytery and General Assembly events?

Think about what is realistic for your church and the youth of your community. In large churches, some programming may need to happen *every day*, whereas in smaller situations, the programming for youth may happen once a month.

Add to each month any other givens from the church calendar— church night suppers, fundraisers, all-church events, retreats, youth events, and other items from the young people's school calendars.

It is very likely in this process that some ideas will surface that may take some extra preparation, such as a series of events, particular events that are large in scope, or special retreats or conferences. Part of the balancing and double checking is to make sure these pieces are spread out across the calendar. It would be difficult to have a big "treasure hunt" one Saturday, a weekend retreat within the next month, a lock-in the next, and then follow that with a four-part series on sexuality. Unless your church or program is huge and there is plenty of leadership for the events, pieces that need a lot of planning or preparation need to be spread out.

These events can be lumped together into a category of special events. These would be any events that don't have a regular weekly or monthly schedule to them.

8. Balancing the Schedule

Ask each of the four groups to take a quarter of the year (a three-month block of time, e.g., September through November) and look at the distribution of the events on the calendar and the other issues discussed above that might need some attention.

Ask them to consider the balance of worship, recreation, mission, and study, estimating the costs of individual events (bowling, skating, mission trips, and miniature golf in each quarter). Discuss these anticipated expenses with the givens already in place on the calendar.

Ask each group to balance their quarter. (They may need to go back to the original brainstorm lists for other ideas.) Provide time for each group to report back to the whole group. At this point it will be necessary to make sure the calendar is balanced over the whole year.

Scheduling

For groups that already have a regular schedule, the next task is to decide which parts of the calendar happen in regularly scheduled events and which need to be special events.

For groups that are beginning or revamping a program, the question is

When can these ideas take place—what is the day of the week, month; and what time frame is needed?

Look at each idea on the calendar and decide when, during the month it is assigned, this idea might take place. How much time is needed for this event?

Other Things to Double-Check

As coordinators of this whole event certain pieces will fall to you to watch for as you move to make this calendar a reality. Questions you may have to ask include the following:

• What leadership is needed for each event?

• What transportation costs or other extraneous expenses must be included?

• How much do these events cost?

• How often are we doing events that cost money?

It may be helpful to go through the list of activities and put a dollar sign ($) next to the events that cost the youth money to participate. If this happens more than once a quarter or even once or twice a year in some situations, this may be too expensive. The program may need some revamping to be more cost conscious and equitable for all. Again, good stewardship must be modeled.

Other related issues are covered in other sections of this book. They are "form" issues—other time or schedule issues, how to make a particular event happen, budget concerns, and so on.

9. Closing

There are several points in this process where the work can be handed over to a smaller group to continue. Therefore it is important to think through how far you want the whole committee to get. At whatever point you close the work, make sure you allow time to pray over what you have accomplished. Close with the group joining in a circle and praying for this process and the year of planning and events to come.

When and Where Should This Program Take Place?

To understand the landscape, prepare by surveying *Exodus 3:1–15.*

When Should Events Happen?

If the program is new and just beginning, the schedule piece of the puzzle cannot be considered until after the planning process has been completed. The schedule and timing pieces are form issues, not function. The planning is a function piece. Since form follows function, we cannot consider schedules and times for events until we know what the needs of the program are.

It would be helpful to think about the goal being to deliver a well-balanced and holistic program of mission, study, worship, and recreation where form follows function. Then, the times for events will become clear.

If you are in a system that has times and schedules that are already set, list these regularly scheduled events for youth and their families on the calendar. These may include Sunday morning church school and Sunday evening Presbyterian Youth Council or youth group meetings. Some churches have regularly scheduled Wednesday evening fellowship or Bible study. Others have a weekly or monthly morning prayer breakfast.

In the purest form of this process, the schedule can "fall out" of the planning. The material developed during the planning process (Chapter 6) will determine the times needed to make these programs and plans happen. This will determine the weekly schedule and will help establish which events are regular and which are special events.

The following questions will help the youth council figure out the times related to the programs developed:

• How much time is needed to do justice to the subject matter?

• In what setting will this subject matter best be explored?

• Are there certain subjects that need to be corrected as a series over a period of time?

The other piece related to timing and schedule is to look at the youth's abilities and needs.

- When are and can the youth be available to be a part of this program?
- What times will be conducive to learning, hearing, experiencing, and understanding the material?

Most youth are not available during the traditional school day. But you may be in an area with year-round schooling or where home-schooling is popular and can plan to have special activities during the non-school times.

Where Should Events Happen?

In the event you have the luxury of building a facility for youth and their families, this is again a "form" issue. As with the scheduling, the program must be lined up before it is possible to know what facilities are needed for which events.

Questions to work with include the following:

- What space is needed to carry out the programs?
- How can this space be designed so that it has multiple uses?
- What space is needed when? Are there different needs at different times of the year?
- What equipment is needed?
- What safety issues need to be considered related to space and activity needs?
- What activities need to be adapted or modified to fit the space that is available?

Visualize the activity. Obviously volleyball can't happen in a small space without adapting the game—but the adapting may be a great and fun idea. On the other hand, a good discussion about the Bible and current events would be fine in a smaller space. In this case, conversation might be enhanced by sitting in comfortable couches or at casual chairs and tables that can easily be moved around. A setting that looks and feels like a traditional school may not be as conducive to open and honest conversation as a setting that feels like a den or an informal living room.

Scheduling the Program

Church school programming and other youth programming need to complement each other. If the programming for church school and the programming for fellowship are not coordinated in some way, they are doomed to encounter some kind of conflict or at least some unnecessary overlap. Overlapping is great when the various aspects complement each other. But the program will seem disjointed if there is conflict because of a lack of planning and intentionality.

After looking at the issues of time and space needed, you may find that the time blocks allotted by a traditional schedule will fit the programming and the youth's schedules. In a traditional schedule, times for regularly scheduled programming for young people have included any one or some combination of the following:

- 45 minutes to an hour every Sunday morning for church school

- 60–90 minutes on Sunday evenings for fellowship, youth group, or Presbyterian Youth Council

- 45–90 minutes during the week for fellowship and study

- 30–45 minutes on a weekday morning for a prayer breakfast

The advantage to Sunday evening programming is that it may be the only day of the week where there is a block of time to manipulate without regard to obligations before or after the time slot. Theoretically, homework is done, dinner can be early or late and at home or church, and youth can be involved in the youth program at church late in the afternoon and still have some evening left for other plans. Youth often can arrange work schedules so they don't have to work on Sunday evenings.

Wednesday or other weekday evenings are a nice planning time, but often school responsibilities don't allow the church programming to begin before 5 P.M. In addition, church activities need to be over early enough so youth can get home for homework or other family responsibilities, and many young people are working jobs that require working on weekday evenings.

There might also be youth or bell choirs or other church responsibilities to throw into this mix. The organizers of these programs must also be included in the scheduling of youth programs. It will help them to know the needs of the youth and understand all the pieces that must be negotiated.

Available leadership is another scheduling issue to be considered. If the youth advisors or the paid youth worker or pastor must work with both the middle school and the senior highs in two separate meetings, they should have some say in the matter. They may be able to do two separate evenings, or maybe a single long evening for both groups would be more convenient.

The pieces to put together here include

- amount of time needed to do the program
- time that the youth have available
- the amount of time available at the facility
- the amount of time appropriate to the day of the week
- other church programming that might have to be integrated
- leadership available for the event

Possible Schedules for Evening Fellowship Options:

A. Middle school/high school meetings on either side of snack supper
5:00 P.M. Middle school
6:00 P.M. Snack supper
6:30 P.M. Senior high
8:00 P.M. Close
B. Simultaneous or broadly graded middle school/high school meeting
6:00 P.M. Snack supper
6:30 P.M. Middle school and high school gatherings
8:00 P.M. Close
C. Fellowship and choir meetings
4:30 P.M. Middle school Presbyterian Youth Council and high school choir
5:30 P.M. Snack
5:45 P.M. High school Presbyterian Youth Council and middle school choir
7:00 P.M. Close—Middle school can have the last one minute as free play

How Do We Really Make It Happen?

To understand the landscape, prepare by surveying *Luke 9:10–17*.

Now you're ready to take the work that has been done, each idea that is now on the calendar, and put it on a Logistics Planning Chart. A chart can be developed for each category of planning—church school, evening youth groups, and special events—and can be organized in several different ways: by activity; by the dates; by days of the week; or by whom is responsible for the event.

For the sake of this conversation, the organization of these activities and the use of the Logistics Planning Chart will first be organized by the kind or category of activity: Presbyterian Youth Council, church school, special events, and so on.

Within the category, the activities need to be listed chronologically. From there go on to fill in the rest of the components of the chart (on the following page). It may also be helpful to put a name in each section of the chart to signify who is responsible for that particular activity or group of activities.

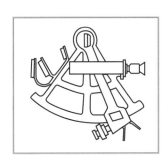

Components of Logistics Planning Chart

Activity: Name of the activity	
Date: Date of the activity	
Time: The time the activity takes place	
Place: Location of the activity	
Setup: How the location should be arranged (tables, chairs, etc.)	
Supplies: The materials needed to make the event happen (balloons, crayons, paper, newsprint, markers, tape, etc.)	
Equipment: Audiovisual and other equipment needed for the event (VCRs, sound systems, jungle gyms, etc.)	
Food: Any food needed for meals (Do not use food if it is not going to be eaten. As good stewards, we should not use food for play unless it will also be eaten.)	
Transportation: Vans or other transportation needed to get youth and from an event (Note if extra drivers are needed for any event.)	
Sponsors: Adults needed to make the event happen (Ideally, there will be one adult for every four middle schoolers and one for every eight senior highs at any given event. For travel trips and conferences there needs to be a one-to-six ratio.)	
P.R.: Publicity done and by whom it is done (How does the word get out about this event? In what forms? How often?)	
Coordinator: The name of the one youth or youth and adults responsible for all these pieces and making sure they get done	

Here is an example of one group's Logistics Planning Chart organized around one activity.

Place:	Church property
Activity:	Treasure Hunt
Time:	11:30 A.M.
Date:	April 11
Coordinators:	Juanita, Tyler
P.R.:	Church bulletin, church newsletter, posters
Sponsors:	Juanita, Joe, Adauri, Kirk
Transportation:	Parents of youth (arranged by coordinators)
Food:	Hot dogs, chips, juice
Supplies:	Prepared clues
Setup:	Pick up litter, establish boundaries, clues

Each of these issues must be dealt with in some way, shape, or form. It *is* possible to get all of this done for any event without filling out the chart. The important issue, though, is making sure someone is responsible for each of these pieces. The youth council and its subcommittees are responsible for making sure all the pieces are covered.

The charts needs to be kept up by the youth council. Each subcommittee of the youth council needs to make sure all this information is taken care of for each event. There will be events for which these charts look quite empty, but there will be other events where a single sheet won't be enough. In most churches, the youth council cochairs are responsible for making sure this information is taken care of or that the charts are filled in. In the event the church has a paid staff person with major responsibilities in youth ministry, this staff person needs to help keep track of this information and/or the charts. If you have a small group and the entire group serves as a council, all youth and adults are responsible for keeping the chart current.

Logistics Planning Chart

PLACE: (location)	
ACTIVITY:	
TIME:	
DATE:	

A C T I V I T Y	**COORDINATOR/S**	
	COSTS: To budget To youth? Adults?	
	PR (PUBLICITY): What? When? By whom?	
E V E N T	**SPONSORS:** How many? Responsibilities?	
	TRANSPORTATION: How? By whom? How many?	
R E S P O N S I B I L I T Y	**FOOD:** Bring? Buy? Order? Supplies?	
	SUPPLIES/AV: Bring? Buy? Order?	
	SET-UPS: Room arrangements	

One should be able to put any activity on this chart and fill in all the categories and see who needs to do what next. If a portion of the chart is not necessary for the activity, put an X through that section to signify that it is not needed.

9

So How Does an Event Happen?

To understand the landscape, prepare yourself by surveying *Luke 6:46–49* and *12:35– 48.*

Flow is everything. Youth need to know they are prepared for and welcomed from the moment they walk in the door. The flow of an event helps involve the youth, set the stage, and move the activities from one to the other in a smooth manner. The flow of activities and the flow within an event can help determine how engaged the youth are in the event and help set the tone for what they get out of an event.

Within any given event, the youth need to be involved in the activities and learnings. One way to look at this is to use "The Five Es"—Engage, Encounter, Explore, Express, and Empower—to help plan the event itself. In any 45- to 90-minute program, or even during a weekend program, these Five Es can take place.

Engage—What happens with the youth when they enter the room? How are they engaged? What leads them to be involved in an event or topic or with other people?

Encounter—How will they first encounter the subject matter? How can this be involving?

Explore—What are ways the youth themselves can explore this subject matter? check out their opinions? explore possible solutions? explore the subject matter in-depth and even experientially?

Express—In what ways can the youth express an opinion on the matters?

Empower—The other Four Es are empty without this piece, which moves us beyond the moment of the particular program. How do we empower the youth to own these new ideas, to be and do what has been learned?

A major underlying assumption in all this is that these Five Es happen within a Christian context. The youth are given opportunities

- to be **engaged** in something Christian
- to **encounter** new ideas and possibilities within this
- to **explore** what that means
- to **express** their opinion about it and/or express a new idea about how the faith comes alive
- to be **empowered** to go and be this person whom Christ calls them to be.

They are empowered to have this all make a difference in their lives. Think through what it is that you want the young people to take home. Every session with the youth has a point. If the point is to have a good time and help them get to know each other, how does this happen? What is done to walk them through the Five Es to make this happen? Take the topic for the event, evening, or program and think about what you want to have happen. Then put the Five Es to work. Ask what activities can happen to help engage the young people in the event and the topic. What needs to happen for them to encounter the subject matter? What activities would allow them to explore their own thoughts on the issues? In what venues can the youth, as individuals and as a group, express their opinions and ideas? And, most important, how can they be empowered to act and/or assimilate new learnings and perspectives into who they are as Christian young people every day?

Another helpful perspective in the planning is for the leaders, youth and adults, to always think: How can these activities and the learnings from these activities be incorporated into everyday life for these young people? These are integration issues. What learnings that happen on the volleyball court can be transferred to everyday life? What does working in a soup kitchen or worship and prayer have to do with our lives as Christians in school? What impact does studying Paul's views on a subject have to do with interactions in after-school programs? The leaders need to watch and encourage young people to explore the "So what?" and "What difference does this make?" issues of youth programming in the church.

10

How and Where Does Church School Fit In?

To understand the landscape, prepare yourself by surveying *Deuteronomy 6:4–9, Proverbs 22:6,* and *Ephesians 6:1–4.*

The term used here is "church school" as opposed to "Sunday school." It may be semantics, but we are helping the youth learn about the church and all that it entails: the church, God, their relationship to Jesus Christ, and how that all manifests itself in the lives of the youth and their families. We are not teaching them about "Sunday."

So the question then is, What *is* the purpose church school? That could be a whole separate book. The youth council needs to answer this question for itself. Church school needs to be a safe place and a comfortable time to explore the life and work of Jesus Christ.

Church school is

• a place to learn about Jesus Christ

• a systematic way of exploring issues related to the faith

• an easy, comfortable, and safe place to learn

• a place to explore and express faith-related issues

Many people are asking, Is Sunday morning the best time for young people to do this kind of learning and be able to explore its applications and implications for life as a Christian today? If church school *is* the time for youth to learn about church and the life and work of Jesus Christ, then we need to explore the best time for young people to do this kind of learning.

In some communities Sunday morning at 9:30 or 9:45 A.M. is the best time for youth to be engaged in this kind of learning. In other communities the church may want to look at different times—a weekday evening? Saturdays? early Sunday afternoons?

If all possibilities of the schedules were considered in the overall planning process done earlier, then it will be possible to pull out those pieces that can happen in a church school setting and implement them within the context of Sunday morning or whatever is the best time to do this kind of continued learning.

An assumption of *all* of this is that programming of all kinds can fall out of the concepts, concerns, and steps listed in this book. Part of the issue is that no one thing can be the only place from which or by which young people come to have a relationship with Jesus Christ and respond to Jesus' call on their lives. Church school is one of several parts.

For some, church school is the place where all of this happens. For others it will be the Sunday or Wednesday night program. For still others it will be special events—be they volleyball games or a mission project—where people can work together. For some it will be any *one* of these places. For others, they will need and use *all* of them.

In any case, the needs of the young people must be held up against the mission of the church, the Vision Statement for Presbyterian Youth Ministry, and/or the Five Intentions of Presbyterian Youth Ministry to assess what is going on and what needs to be happening.

How Do We Communicate Our Plans?

To understand the landscape, prepare yourself by surveying *Proverbs 1:5*.

Do not assume there is good communication about programming between the youth and their families. When working on any kind of communications, address the material to the youth *and* their families. Think about your language: "youth and their parents" may not fit if the youth in your church come from the Presbyterian Home in your area, but "youth and their families" may be appropriate.

Think through which pieces will need to go to youth only, to parents only, and to youth and their families. In smaller churches, all notices of any kind can be addressed to both parties. In larger churches, it may be more practical to have separate pieces for parents/families and for youth. In any case, parents *must* be connected to the program through its communications. Programming is not helped if it tries to separate itself or the youth from their families. If we are talking about holistic programming, we are talking about communicating with those with whom the youth live also. We need to encourage the involvement of parents and families in the scheduling and prioritizing of the young person's time.

Communication and public relations depend on the **Five Ws** and **Two Hs**

Who?
What?
When?
Where?
Why?
How?
How much?

This information needs to be in most every piece that goes out to youth and their families. The youth and the family need this much detail, and the rest of the church will be better able to support the ministry if they know what is behind the program and can see what its purpose is.

> *From an older adult in the church who is not directly involved with the youth program:*
> *"Your article in the church newsletter did not say why you were doing a fundraiser. I would be glad to contribute to the fundraiser, but not without knowing why you are raising money."*

The Church's Attention Span: Four Months

Individuals and families need information far in advance so they can plan for and support activities in the life of the church and youth program.

Major events that are a part of the regularly scheduled program or that are special events need to be on the church calendar and on family calendars far enough in advance so that they make the priority list. There is so much that competes for the time youth can give to any project or commitment that having events on the calendar with plenty of advanced notice is imperative.

In addition to planning ahead, if the event is major the church needs to be reminded about it several times. Announcing a major early spring mission project in September is great, but without reminders, the church will forget about it by Christmas.

Four Weeks ➡➡ Two Weeks ➡➡ One Week

Think about this kind of formula when it comes to publicity for any event. Four weeks before the event, the youth and their families need to know about the details (who, what, when, where, why, how, and how much). Each week after this and until the event, they need some kind of reminder. Two weeks before, they need an update on the details. The week before, they need the "last-minute hurrah" and push to encourage participation.

Communication/Work Calendar/Chart

Here again, this comes from the "form follows function" method of planning.

✓ Twelve to fifteen months ahead—get the concept going

✓ Four to six months ahead—while committees and/or individuals are working on the details, get it on the family calendar. Send invitation if it is camp/conference-type event with information about the importance of "RSVPing" and/or registering.

✓ Four months ahead—plant seeds about the "big stuff"
✓ Four to five weeks ahead—start major publicity; send appropriate invitations
✓ Within the month ahead—weekly reminders
✓ Week before—last big push and calls made

Time before event	Work to be done on the event/idea	Publicity timeline
12–15 months	Get the concept going	If sessional approval is needed, do this now (e.g., mission trip)
4–6 month out	Details need to be developed	Event needs to be on church and family calendars, including general information on how to RSVP and/or register
4 months out	Individual and group work on details continues	Plant the seeds. Major details (the five Ws and two Hs) need to be publicized, in a special mailing if necessary
4 weeks out	Finalize details	Major publicity push and reminders; details in newsletter
2 weeks before	Give an update on details	Mailings, phone trees, church bulletins
1 week before	Follow-up calls made	Final encouragement; article in guide to worship; meeting times and place
Day before	Final details	
1 week after	Thank you notes sent	

It is possible to scale this down to suit a particular situation. This gives details about the flow of information.

The Look of Publicity Pieces

Producing eye-catching publicity pieces is particularly necessary with youth. This does *not* mean all material needs to be slick and look like it came from TV or a hip magazine, but it does mean youth must be able to read the information at a glance. This can be as simple as making a few key words or phrases **bold** within the text. Details can follow.

Straight text rarely works. People will look for straight text to help answer questions, but if you want to get them interested so they will start *asking* questions, something has to attract their attention.

This can be done in several ways—a mix of "clip art" or simple drawings (even stick figures) with a few different type sizes and fonts will pull the reader's eye into the material.

Publicity can take place in the weekly church bulletin or newsletter, but some supplemental information needs to be added also:

- phone calls, invitations, even reminder messages left on answering machines can encourage attendance and keep people informed

- special mailings—some just for youth and some for youth and their families

- announcements at regularly scheduled events (during church, during other youth programs, etc.)

Also, passing conversations, where you mention to a young person that you hope they will be at church school, or hope they are going on the mission trip, make youth aware that you care about their participation.

There is no one way that is effective for all youth. The only thing true for all youth when it comes to communicating events and schedules is that they all need lots of encouragement and all need to hear an invitation or to hear about an opportunity more than once. Think about it—this is true for people of all ages.

Conversely, guilt goes nowhere! Pressure tactics don't work for most young people. They may work periodically, but will, in the long run, cause resentment. Young people can tell the difference between when they are being pressured or manipulated to attend and when they are wanted and welcomed.

Other Publicity Ideas

- Prepare a newsletter for youth and their parents to be sent monthly, or at least two to four times a year. One page (8.5" x 11") is a great size.

- Encourage the *youth* to write their own newsletter monthly or at least a few times a year.

- Encourage the youth to write newsy articles of youth events for the church's newsletter.

- Divide up the names of the youth in the church among the youth council. Have the council send special greetings at random times of the year. During mid-term exams or "We love our youth" week (you decide when that is) is a good time. Regular birthday greetings are great too.
- Make sure information going to the youth is addressed to them personally.
- Make sure parents are informed of all youth events. A parent newsletter that has youth events and details listed is important. A section on parenting is helpful and is always appreciated.
- If a church cannot afford (in time or money) to put out separate parent and youth newsletters, or any newsletter, it is imperative that the information going to youth include parent information or at least be addressed to "Youth and their parents."

It is also extremely helpful to have a parent/youth meeting at the beginning of the year to get all the parents on board with the plans for the year. This can be a purely informative time or it can be a way of building community (youth to parents, parents to parents, and youth to youth).

A parent/youth meeting can

- help disseminate the youth calendar for the quarter or the year;
- go over special event details, that is, mission project details, conference sign-up information, retreat needs;
- build community and understanding between youth and youth, youth and adults, and parents and parents; and
- solicit parent help for particular events, such as hosts for progressive dinners, drivers for events, extra chaperons for retreats, and cooks for special events.

⟨12⟩

How Do We Pay for All This?

To understand the landscape, prepare yourself by surveying *Matthew 25:14–30;* and *Luke 12:32–34.*

When it comes to money and budgeting for youth ministry, if "form is to follow function," then any budget information should also fall out of the planning that has been done. Budget is a part of the "form" that youth ministry's functions present. There are several bits of information to consider that can help with at least a minimal amount of budgeting.

A church leader once challenged a group to think back to their earliest memory of money—Where did it come from? What was it used for? How did you get it? This is a great concept to keep in mind: In dealing with money we are teaching young people concepts of stewardship and helping them develop principles for how they work with and what they think about money.

But it is helpful to first look at how the rest of the church is structured and how that budgeting process functions. If the church is under a "unicameral" system, fundraisers may not be possible. Often the unicameral system assumes that the church community is asked for money *once* during the year. The stewardship campaign is comprehensive. All needs are listed and explained during the annual stewardship drive.

What does this do for youth ministry?

- It means that all this planning will pay off. The youth and their families and the rest of the church community will know what and when something is being done and know ahead of time the financial needs of all programming. When the church commits to the whole church's stewardship program, it is committing to the youth portion of this whole.

- It means that this is a great opportunity to help youth learn about their part in stewardship, because their programming is obviously included in the rest of the church's ministry. As the rest of the church learns about the opportunities for service, the youth piece is within that.

- It means there can be no fundraising without sessional approval. Often this means that the session will not allow fundraising of any kind.

In any system it is important to have sessional approval. Any fundraising can have issues related to church policy and even legal matters. It is imperative to keep the church informed about the youth council's intentions of dealing with money. The session is responsible for confirming the budgets of all church functions, and this is one of them.

Now look again at the lists of activities to do for the year or look at the calendar of events from the planning process. Put a $ beside each item that costs money. To get a bit more detailed and elaborate, devise a rating system of some kind.

> **$** = cost is minimal (uses only supplies available at church)
> **$$** = cost of some additional supplies and/or equipment
> **$$$** = cost is enough to warrant charging the youth a sum

Look at the categories from which these pieces come. Total each category's expenses. These totalled together can help develop the budget for the youth program.

Look at these categories developed in the planning and programming. These alone can also become the line items for the budget. Totalling the costs within each category can become the budget for the youth program. Some line items will have no expenses. These can be dropped from the budget lines if they are forecast to have no future expense.

There may be some pieces that are big enough that they will need their own line items. Camp and conference expenses are a good example of this. Any overnight events and events of length that are places of growth, learning, outdoor adventure, and community building can be put together in one line item. This would include retreats, camps, and conferences.

One major piece that might not manifest itself in the planning process is leadership development. This is a necessary piece to help develop leadership within the youth program. This is for youth and adults—separately and together! Some of this might happen for individuals through reading books and self-taught learning. Much of it can happen through local presbytery, synod, and General Assembly training events. These events happen quarterly, biannually, and annually. It is worth a call to the local presbytery and synod offices to find out what is available in your area. General Assembly youth events happen at various places around the country and at the Montreat Conference Center in Montreat, North Carolina.

In figuring the cost of events per person, there are several questions that must be dealt with. These may also be questions and conversations that can lead to establishing some guidelines for how some programming is developed and how the youth budget is determined.

- How much and how often do the youth pay out of their own pocket? To ask youth today to pay for an event more than once or twice a year is asking too much. It is possible to do good programming that is paid for or at least subsidized by the church's youth budget. Weekend events, retreats, purely recreational events, and camps and conferences may be the exceptions to this. Fundraising and *FUN*raising guidelines may help with this issue too. They are discussed later.

- Which expenses of the adult leaders should the church/youth budget be paying? A portion, if not all, of an adult advisor's expenses should be paid for most any event. Since these people are on duty and responsible for the youth, the least the church can do is to help pay for any events that cost money. In the event of a retreat or a conference, the adult chaperons and advisors are on duty twenty-four hours a day. In most instances, all of their expenses should be paid. The exceptions to this might be events that are purely recreational. In these cases, the adults should have to pay for a portion of their fun too.

Other examples of line items that can go in a budget might include the following:

Church school curriculum
Sunday evening youth group
Leader development training
Subscriptions and gifts
Camps and conferences
Supplies
Equipment
Transportation
Childcare for youth advisors

Fundraisers

Each youth council needs guidelines for fundraising. Without guidelines, raising money can feel like nickel and diming the church and community and can begin to dictate other aspects of programming. Written guidelines for raising money for the youth program need to be developed and adopted by the youth council and passed on to the session for approval. With guidelines written, the youth will be more interested in investing their time and energy and the members of the church will often be more open to participating and giving. They then understand what the monies are doing for the youth and others. This kind of understanding can help broaden and encourage participation too. This is what I refer to as "FUNderstanding."

If we take seriously scriptural guidelines and the ideas of stewardship, money should never be raised for self-serving interests. Monies raised need to be for the good of the larger church in some way. Money can be raised with these concepts in mind:

• the Five Intentions and/or the vision statement;
• the good of the youth as related to their faith journeys; and
• the good of the church.

Priorities and guidelines can be established easily from these. Therefore, if the group is constantly raising money for recreational events, for example, there are at least two sets of concerns: Why is the program purely recreational, and what benefit is this giving the youth? What are we teaching them about money?

It can also add some merriment to raising money by adding language that will make publicity related to fundraising fun to read and appealing to youth. This also helps with the old attitudes of fundraising being free handouts.

A couple of "sniglets" that can be helpful:

✔ **FUNraising**—Our way of raising fun and money to help others.

✔ **FUNderstanding**—What we do to help the youth and the rest of the congregation understand about the *fun* being raised and where the *funds* raised will go.

Basic guidelines of fundraising should include
1. Ways of raising money to help subsidize the youth budget
2. Service to others in some way.

Monies raised from fundraising
1. Will benefit youth who participated in the fundraisers
2. Will be held in a reserved or restricted account until needed for a particular event

3. Will not be used on purely recreational events

The youth council must elaborate on these and tailor them to each particular situation. There are other conversations that must happen or questions that must be answered among the youth council members related to money, budgets, and fundraising. For example:

If there are unspent monies, can they be rolled over into a reserved account?

What do fundraisers pay for in youth activities? Do they cover all events? If so, how much? (all expenses for all participants? only those who participated in the fundraisers? only the adults? only part of the actual cost?) Do they subsidize only mission projects?

My Favorite Fundraiser Ideas

For most any fundraisers of this kind, it is helpful for the youth, their budget, and the giver of the money if donations are taken. This frees up more people to give more and enables different kinds of monetary gifts.

Fellowship Events

• Potluck meal, cake auction, entertainment

• Variety show hosted by the youth (open to all members of the church)

• Potato and salad bar lunch

Car Washes

Live Christmas Cards

"Cards" available to be purchased and delivered as gifts. A card is

• a bouquet of balloons (on sticks is cheaper than helium)

• a homemade card with a personal greeting from the giver

• a basket of goodies—inexpensive candies or goodies made by the youth in used baskets collected from people in the church (a request for used, but good, baskets in the church newsletter can reap great benefits)

• Christmas carols or a brief skit

To "make" the cards:

1. Check with a local flower shop or balloon delivery service

for the cost of a bouquet delivery. Price the Live Cards under the price of the commercial deliveries.

2. Set times for deliveries. Certain times on a Saturday, Sunday afternoon or evening, or after-school hours often work best.

3. Take orders for deliveries. Get the name of the giver; the name, address, and phone number of the receiver; a greeting from the giver; the time they want the "card" delivered; and their check.

4. The giver must be responsible for the receiver being home at the time of the delivery.

The day before delivery, the youth

make up the cards;

rehearse the delivery (singing, skit, etc.)

prepare the balloons; and

set the delivery routes and prepare anything else.

On the delivery, ring the doorbell and begin singing (a la Christmas caroling). When the people answer the door, identify yourselves: "We are the youth of Preston Hollow Presbyterian and we have a Live Christmas Card for the Moores from the Odoms. Are you the Moores? If you have a minute, we'd like to (sing a couple of carols, share a Christmas skit, etc.) for you."

Then hand them the balloons, the basket of goodies, and the card, and do the three to five minutes of entertainment (if applicable). Wish them Merry Christmas, in song if you like, and move on to the next house.

Live Cards can be done at other times of the year for other celebrations.

Babysitting

Babysitting so parents can go out is often an effective fundraiser. Open the church nursery for babysitting so that parents can have dinner out or go shopping for a holiday. This is especially effective on the several Saturdays before Christmas. It might also work on a Friday or Saturday evening on or near Valentine's Day.

◄ **13** ►

Survey These Plots of Land

To understand the landscape, prepare yourself by surveying *John 15:1–17, 1 Corinthians 12,* and *2 Corinthians 4:7–16.*

What is it we are trying to do with youth? To answer in a nutshell—We are about helping make the gospel come alive today, right now, for young people! For Presbyterians and most youth ministries, that can happen through the Five Intentions and the Vision Statement, and these pieces of youth ministry take on wings through the gospel.

What are we doing here? The youth issues we are "surveying" are

Identity: We are helping young people discover who they are and whose they are. We want each young person to better understand what it means to be a child of God and to know that they belong to God.

Belonging: Youth need to know they have a place in the life of the church and are a part of the community of faith.

The following can be manifested in these two issues for youth ministry:

Decision-Making Skills: Offering young people the chance to see the world through the lenses of Christ.

Leadership Development: Encouraging youth to be leaders today, as members of the church. This is their responsibility and a calling.

Conversion Experiences: Opportunities to see and experience faith in action on a firsthand basis is a part of all youth ministry. Otherwise we are just another program for youth. Youth need to see what it means to be a part of the church now.

Relating Faith to Life: In our increasingly secular society, it is more and more important for youth to see, experience, and understand what it means to be a Christian today. Unfortunately, it is possible to compartmentalize our society so that church and faith issues happen only on Sunday or only at church. In any activity or event we do with youth we need to be asking them, So what? What difference does this make? What do we learn from what we do at church? What does it do for us tomorrow and in our lives?

Some of these plots of land in youth ministry might look like these:

What youth ministry is happening here?
Every two weeks the group of three youth and one adult get together to do what they've planned: a movie and Bible-study discussion, a game, a hike and an outdoor worship, an afternoon at the local food bank.

What youth ministry is happening here?
In this church of 150, a young man sits on the Christian Education Committee when it meets each month. Each quarter he shares what the youth group of eight has planned for the following months. He is asked his opinion on church school curriculum and possible teachers for all ages.

What youth ministry is happening here?
The youth council meets monthly to have reports from the subcommittees and discuss the details of the coming month. This group of eighteen is cochaired by the adult elder and a youth. The youth cochair position rotates in January and June of each year.

What youth ministry is happening here?
After a great game of volleyball, the group sits down and talks about where and how God is in the game and the play. They discuss the church and God's movement in all of their lives: in their play, worship, study, and service with the church. They are realizing that an afternoon with others from church can be a microcosm of everything they do: all of life, learning for the future, and living it today also.

What youth ministry is happening here?
There are two youth in the church. On Sunday mornings, they teach in the children's church school. Periodically they are liturgists in Sunday worship. On Wednesday mornings they meet for morning prayers with their youth advisor. Once a month they meet with other area church youth for fellowship.

What youth ministry is happening with and for youth where you are?

Surveying the land in youth ministry has many components. The landscape is diverse and beautiful, reflecting God's grace and goodness. The individual plots of land in youth ministry come in many shapes and sizes and are at various stages of development. Now you have some additional tools and resources to begin, enhance, or support youth ministry in your area.

Appendix

Youth/Leader Events

1. Call your local presbytery, synod, general conference, or association offices for listings of youth/leader events in your area.

2. Contact
   Montreat Conference Center
   P.O. Box 969
   Montreat, NC 28757
   704/669-2911 x336
   800/572-2257 x336
   800-811-9098 (24 hours) for brochures

3. Contact
   Presbyterian Youth Ministry Office
   100 Witherspoon Street
   Louisville, KY 40202-1396
   502-569-5499

4. Continuing Education Event for Youth Ministry Professionals—First or second weekend in January

5. Association of Presbyterian Church Educators (APCE)—End of first full week of February

6. Presbyterian Youth Triennium—Centrally located in the United States. Held every three years (1998, 2001, etc.)

7. Presbyterian Youth Connection Events—Every three years the summer before Trienniums (1997, 2000, etc.)

The Presbyterian Youth Connection

The Five Intentions of Presbyterian Youth Ministry:
1. To call young people to be disciples in Jesus Christ
2. To respond to the needs and interests of young people
3. To work together, youth and adults, in partnership
4. To be connected to the whole church, community, world
5. To include all young people, reaching out and inviting them to belong to the community of faith

A Vision Statement for Youth Ministry in the Presbyterian Church (U.S.A.)

Adopted by the 202nd General Assembly (1990) of the Presbyterian Church (U.S.A.)

As those involved in youth ministry, young people and adults, this is our vision . . .

We are children of God.
We are female and male, of all ages and conditions.

We come from many social, economic, and racial/ethnic backgrounds. As God's children, we are called into a loving relationship with our Creator, Redeemer, and Sustainer.

We experience God's love as the Holy Spirit leads us in the living of life.

We are Presbyterians.
We are part of the Reformed family of faith.

We experience God's love and grace through prayer, worship, service, the study of scripture and history, our participation in the church as the body of Christ, our partnership with people of other faiths, and our ministry of seeking justice for all people.

We are a vital part of the church and its mission. Through youth ministry, we are nurtured as the church responds to our needs and interests and as we give and share ourselves in the church's mission and ministry.

We have a vision of youth ministry in the church . . .
Where each young person is called to be
a disciple of Jesus Christ and is helped to
grow in a dynamic, genuine and meaningful faith;

Where young people are involved throughout
the church's life and are able to take risks in a supportive community
without fear of rejection;

Where young people are educated within their congregations and in institutions both secular and sacred, and are supported in their quest for truth and knowledge in all disciplines;

Where youth and adults together as partners create a community which celebrates diversity and cherishes each other's gifts;

Where youth are challenged and enabled to respond to God's call to wholeness in their lives and in the world; and

Where young people discover and claim over and over again the Good News of God's redeeming and sustaining love.

Vision gives direction to all ministry.
"Where there is no vision, the people will perish." — *Proverbs 29:18.*

Without vision, youth ministry becomes lifeless.
This vision, which we claim, seeks wholeness and life for all children of God.

Bibliography

Roland Martinson. *Effective Youth Ministry*. Nashville: Augsburg, 1988.
Cultural and developmental issues, congregation based, some activities

Donald Ng, ed. *Asian Pacific American Youth Ministry*. Judson Press, 1988.
Culture, family, theology, history, trends, programs

Wayne Rice. *Up Close and Personal*. Youth Specialties, 1989.
Group building ideas and activities, programs listed need help

Karl Rohnke. *Bottomless Bag, Again?* Project Adventure, Kendall/Hunt Publishing, 1995.

———. *Bottomless Baggie*. Project Adventure, Kendall/Hunt Publishing, 1995.

———. *Quicksilver*. Project Adventure, Kendall/Hunt Publishing, 1995.
Games and activities. Must add faith issues and debriefing

Denny Rydberg. *Youth Group Trust Builders*. Loveland, CO: Group, 1993.
Activities for community building, some take equipment

Thom and Joani Schultz. *Kids Taking Charge: Youth-led Youth Ministry*. Loveland, CO: Group, 1991.
Good how-to book, basics and start-up issues, not much long-range info

Michael Warden. *Small Church Youth Ministry Programming Ideas*. Loveland, CO: Group, 1994.
All kinds of ideas for the small church and/or small youth group

Getting Connected: Presbyterian Youth Connection Congregational Guide. A Presbyterian Youth Connection Resource. Louisville, KY: Presbyterian Church (U.S.A.), 1996.
Planning helps, theological basis for youth ministry, ways of organizing using the Five Intentions. To order call 1-800-524-2612 and request PDS #70-250-96-206.

Guidebook for Presbyterian Youth Ministry. Louisville, KY: Geneva Press, 1988.
Overall guide, how-tos, PC(USA) info, Five Intentions, resources

The Playbook. Maness, Shackelford, Washburn.
Resource games and other group related activities. Good for all ages. To order call 1-800-333-2772.

PYC Program Designs: 20 Designs for 6th–8th Grade Youth Groups. A Presbyterian Youth Connection Resource. Louisville, KY: PC(USA), 1996.
Includes tips and articles for leaders and twenty programs for youth. Relevant and fun! To order call 1-800-524-2612 and request PDS #70-250-96-207.

PYC Program Designs: 20 Designs for 9th–12th Grade Youth Groups. A Presbyterian Youth Connection Resource. Louisville, KY: PC(USA), 1996.
Includes tips and articles for leaders and twenty programs for senior highs. Great hot topics!
To order call 1-800-524-2612 and request PDS #70-250-96-208.

Presbyterian Youth Connection Leader. Louisville, KY: PC(USA).
Quarterly publication, free!

The Kid's Multicultural Art Book: Hands Around the World. Williamson Publishing